How to Bond Rabbits - a Practical Guide

First edition 2017, revised August 2017
Printed by CreateSpace, An Amazon.com Company

ISBN 978-1545415993

Copyright © 2017 Rebekka Faial

All rights reserved. No part of this publication may be reproduced or transmitted in any form or by any means without permission in writing from the author.

Illustrations: Bowie Rain
Front and back cover: Pixabay

"How to Bond Rabbits — a Practical Guide" has been published to assist rabbit owners in understanding the best approaches to bonding rabbits. The suggestions are only intended as a complement to common sense and your own knowledge of your rabbits and what is best for them. The author takes no responsibility for any injury suffered by any rabbit owner or rabbit.

Table of content

Introduction 1

The Social Life of Rabbits 2
   Life in the warren 2
   The hierarchy of wild rabbits 4
   The hierarchy of pet rabbits 7

Body Language 8

Before You Get Started 10
   Do your groundwork 10
   How age and sex affect bonding 11
   Neutering 12
   Unacceptable behaviour 13
   When are they bonded 15

Let the Bonding Begin 16
   The stress-free bonding 16
   The classic bonding 18
   The stress bonding 21
   Bonding multiple rabbits 22

When Nothing Goes as Planned 24

Bonding with Your Rabbit 26

Frequently Asked Questions 27

Dedicated to all the beautiful four-legged friends who have filled my life and heart with joy.

Introduction

When you picked up this book, it was probably because you have decided you want your rabbit to have a friend. Great! Rabbits are social animals, and they are happier and healthier when they share their lives with other rabbits. Research has even confirmed that rabbits that live with other rabbits have better immunity to diseases and are more relaxed. Even if research did not so clearly tell us that a rabbit is better off when it has a rabbit friend, rabbit owners all over the world know from first hand that rabbits become more lively and content once a rabbit friend moves in.

Once you have seen two rabbits spend the day together, eating together, sleeping together, grooming each other, playing together, and even using the litter box together, you will know how much it means to them to have a companion. Rabbits are social animals, but they are also protective of their territory. With the best of intentions, many rabbit owners have tried to put two rabbits that did not know each other at all in the same cage, and have been shocked to see the rabbits attack each other fiercely. Such stories have frightened many owners into believing that it is difficult and even impossible to bond rabbits and it is better to keep them separated. The good news is that bonding rabbits is quite easy, if you know a thing or two about rabbit behavior.

Throughout the years I have bonded so many rabbits, I have lost count, and I have helped even more rabbit owners with practical tips and support. All my experience from the many years of researching, studying rabbit behavior and helping rabbit owners is the basis for this practical guide. With this book I want to help you bond your rabbits. I want you to enjoy the bonding process and find it exciting. I hope to teach you about natural rabbit behavior, give you insight into why your rabbits react as they do, and provide you with practical advice on different ways to bond your rabbits.

This book assumes that you already have basic knowledge about rabbit care and neutering. You will for that reason not find any information about rabbit care. I only offer a practical guide to bonding rabbits. The book is written with the responsible and loving rabbit owner in mind who already knows that these wonderful animals need a great deal of space in order to be happy and healthy. If you have been keeping your rabbits primarily in a cage or run, improve your rabbits' living conditions before you begin the bonding process.

- Rebekka

The Social Life of Rabbits

There are 28 species of wild rabbits around the world. The best-known and most recognizable of the 28 rabbit species is the European rabbit (Oryctolagus cuniculus). The rabbits we love and care for in our homes are all domesticated descendants of the European rabbit. While the European rabbit is the best-known species, it is probably also the least typical of the species. The European rabbit constructs the most extensive burrow systems, called warrens, while many of the other species make surface nests. The European rabbit is also the most social rabbit, often forming groups in warrens of up to 20 individuals, yet it is even seen that up to hundreds of individuals live together. Most other rabbit species are relatively solitary coming together only to breed or occasionally to forage in small groups. Although rabbits have been kept as pets for hundreds of years, we can still see traces of their wild ancestors when it comes to behavior and instincts. Especially their social side. We can understand our pet rabbits much better by getting to know their wild ancestor.

Living in close quarters not only fulfils the gregarious rabbits' needs for close, physical contact and company, but it also helps them stay healthy. Mutual grooming is a big part of their everyday lives. Grooming serves a very practical purpose for the rabbits — mutual grooming is a way to keep each others' fur clean and free of parasites as well as it calms them and lowers stress. It is also a friendly gesture that creates a bond between the many rabbits. By grooming each other, the group becomes more closely knit, which increases their chance of survival. Life is dangerous and often short for a wild rabbit. Rabbits are prey animals. Living in a warren with other rabbits helps protect them from predators, as there is always one or more rabbits nearby to give a warning if a predator gets close. A prey animal that lives alone will need to be constantly on the lookout for predators. That is a difficult task for a rabbit that also need to eat and sleep once in a while.

Life in the warren
The size of a warren can vary from a single pair up to hundreds of rabbits. Each warren is a complex labyrinth of interconnecting tunnels running off in all directions containing living quarters, nesting areas, bolt runs and emergency exits that the rabbits use if a predator is in the area. The living quarters are made up of small and large chambers that serve various purposes. The many

tunnels crisscross in several levels to help protect the rabbits from any predators that might find their way in. A large warren can have more than 50 entrances and exits. Some entrances are easy to see from the outside, while others are hidden, quick escape routes for a rabbit, yet difficult for a predator to fit into. While most of the tunnels are very narrow — about 15 cm (5,9 in) in diameter — there are also wider tunnels of about 40 cm (15.75 in) in diameter where the rabbits can pass each other. A big warren can easily be three meters deep and stretch over an area as big as a tennis court. The rabbits like to keep close to each other, and stay close to their homes — they rarely venture more than 200 meters (656 ft.) away from the main burrow.

As the warren grows, it divides into smaller social groups. Space quickly becomes cramped after mating season, which means it will soon be time for young rabbits to move away from the family. Female rabbits usually stay, while young male rabbits move to a new group in the warren or perhaps find a new warren. If they do not find a warren to move into, the young male rabbits may make a home at the outer edges of an existing warren. Although their contact with the other rabbits is minimal, they still enjoy the protection of the warren without actually being a part of it.

New warrens and colonies are usually created by a female rabbit at the bottom of the hierarchy when she digs a nest for her litter. Being at the bottom of the hierarchy means she does not have access to the best nesting chambers at the center of the warren. Instead, she builds her nest in a separate burrow in the warren, called a stop. The stop can be a separately dug burrow, which may eventually become starting point of a new colony.

The hierarchy of wild rabbits

In all rabbit colonies over a certain size, you will find a social hierarchy. The social hierarchy represents the established order in the warren and is the best means for any social animals to live closely together without constantly fighting over food or mates. The rabbits with the highest position in the social hierarchy get access to all the available resources, breed succesfully and remain alive even under critical environmental situations. The social hierarchy in the warren is upheld by various factors such as the number of rabbits in the warren, the access to resources, etc.

On top of the social hierarchy in a rabbit warren you find a male with one or several mates. When a rabbit is at the top of the hierarchy, we call the rabbit dominant. That word may have a negative ring to it, but in this context "dominant" simply means that the rabbit has a higher social status compared to other rabbits. Among the other rabbits in the warren, there are various groupings. Most have a mate and a group they belong to. A rabbit hierarchy is not a pyramidal hierarchy. It is best explained as a star-shaped hierarchy with overlapping groups, each of which has a dominant rabbit. Each overlapping group has its own hierarchy that is part of the larger hierarchy. To make it more complex, a larger warren also often has a number of rabbits that do not belong to one group or the other. These rabbits come and go between the groups.

Male and female rabbits are not part of the same hierarchy; they each have their own social grouping, which means that conflicts between male and female rabbits are rare. In fact, fights between rabbits in a warren are usually not common, because of the somewhat stable hierarchy.

Marking the territory

The dominant male constantly patrols his territory. On his patrols, he makes sure everything is as it should be and that there is enough space and resources for everyone. If resources are limited, he will chase the young male rabbits out, so they can move into a new warren (usually one nearby). When he is patrolling, the dominant male rabbit also marks his territory by leaving scent marks from his anal glands, as well as the scent glands located under his chin. He is not the only one to mark the territories, though. The females mark their nests by spraying urine. Under the ground everything is dark and so scent marking is an effective way to communicate with other rabbits.

Researchers have not yet determined why one particular rabbit is awarded the status as the dominant rabbit in the group, but some studies suggest it is genetically determined. Rabbits with large scent glands seem to have higher social status. The larger scent glands make it easier for them to cover up another rabbit's scent markings and that way claim a territory. Another study has shown that males birthed by the dominant female rabbit tend to be granted a high status. This might have something to do with the advantages that are part of their upbringing. Probably other factors play a role too, but these are still unknown to us.

Ritualized aggression

The social hierarchy ensures that the rabbits live together peacefully most of the time. Fights can break out though if the dominant male is weakened and a new male wants to challenge him to take his position, mates and territory. During the mating season, however, both male and female rabbits become more territorial. Male rabbits will chase away other males who try to mate with their mate(s), while females will protect their chosen nesting chamber from other females. A good nest is located in the middle of the warren, so during mating season females at the bottom of the hierarchy are kept away by the more dominating females, who want to protect the best nests from being taken.

Fights between female rabbits in the warren are rare, and between the male rabbits, it is mostly a case of chasing each other away. That said, physical confrontations between rabbits do occur — whether they are about nests, mates, or status — but rabbits do their best not to injure each other. Instead, they use "ritualized aggression", usually seen as digging or jumps to show their physical superiority. By showing off their physical superiority an actual fight between the rivals can be avoided. Ritualized aggression is normal between social animals. It is a way to solve conflicts without weakening the group or physically harming each other. When animals show ritualized aggression, they display a series of escalating threatening behaviors that can end with physical contact between the rivals. But the display rarely leads to serious injuries. Usually, the rival will retreat before the situation escalates to an actual fight. The outcome of a showdown between two rabbits is not always decided by physical ability, social status or scent glands. In most cases, the rabbit that "owned" the territory in the first place comes out as the winner. A study has shown that rabbits "win" 80% of the time, if they own the territory in the first place. We see the same tendency in other social animals. Those with the most to lose will always be more threatening in their behavior and will feel more self-confident on their home territory.

The level of aggression among the rabbits depends on several factors, such as the size of the warren and the number of available escape routes. Rabbits living in crowded colonies are less tolerant than rabbits living in colonies with abundance of food and space. If resources are limited, the level of aggression and territorial behavior is higher seeing that the rabbits are fighting to survive.

The mating season

The mating season for wild rabbits usually lasts from February until June, but varies. Around December and January, the male rabbits' testicles begin to descend, and both sexes begin to be interested in mating. The male rabbits change temperament in the mating season. They chase other male rabbits away if they come too close to their female mate(s). The female rabbits begin to defend the best nesting chambers in the warren. During the days up to the birth of a litter, the female rabbit can be very territorial to ensure that other females do not take her nesting chamber from her. Although rabbits are generally social creatures, they spend most of the mating season primarily only with their mates.

By June, the male rabbits' testicles retract to their abdomen again, so they can no longer breed (male rabbits are actually able to retract their testicles at any time, and often do so when they are frightened or about to fight another male. It is a very effective way of protecting the testicles). Now that the mating season is over, the social structure of the warren changes entirely as the hormone levels fall to normal. The rabbits once again spend time together in the large chambers under the ground, and their normal peaceful, social life resumes.

The hierarchy of pet rabbits

Our beloved pet rabbits are very similar to their wild cousins. They too form a hierarchy when they live together with other rabbits, and are social, gregarious animals. Few rabbit owners keep more than two rabbits, however, and with such a small number, your rabbits have no need to establish a hierarchy. Only when several rabbits of the same sex live together will you see that a hierarchy is being established.

Most rabbit owners have a male and a female rabbit. As you know now, female and male rabbits do not share the same hierarchy, although they can certainly fight if there is a lack of food or space. In this case, it is not about status. Instead they fight due to stress or a- often seen in caged rabbits - basic survival instinct because of limited space.

Even though our domesticated rabbits do not need to establish a hierarchy among themselves, there can still be times during the bonding process where we can see them using "ritualized aggression" by digging, running at each other, lifting their tails, jumping, etc.

Pet rabbits do not have the same defined mating season as wild rabbits do. Many of them are fertile year-round, and so their behavior is similar to that of the wild rabbits during mating season. Although that makes our pet rabbits quite territorial, the good news is that studies have shown that domesticated rabbits are much less aggressive than wild rabbits — although our pet rabbits can certainly come off as very aggressive if they have not been neutered. When our rabbits are neutered, they will display the same unreserved and sociable behavior as wild rabbits outside of mating season.

Body Language

Our rabbits communicate much more than we realize. Rabbit language is mostly silent and consists of a lot of small signals. They communicate through their body language.

When bonding rabbits, it is important that you are able to read their body language. Look carefully at your rabbit's ears and tail, which will tell you a lot about what is happening — and what might happen in a few seconds. The position of a rabbit's ears shows its mood. Just a small change in the direction of the ears can signal the difference between a curious rabbit and one that is ready to attack.

Relaxed rabbit

Curious

Nervous/aggressive

Alert

Relaxed/sleeping

When a rabbit is relaxed, its ears lie flat against its back. If the ears are upright, the rabbit is alert. When a rabbit is investigating something unknown and potentially dangerous, it moves slowly forward. The rabbit stretches its body and might move the front part of its body forward and backwards to get close to what it wants to investigate. Its back legs remain put, so it can quickly run away again. A rabbit investigating something does not hop; it walks. Slowly. Its ears will point forward, and its head will be stretched. This type of behavior is often seen when two rabbits that do not know each other meet. It is a sign of curiosity. A good sign. The body language for curiosity and a potential attack are unfortunately almost identical, but there is a small, crucial difference that it is important to recognize: If a rabbit is ready to attack, its ears will be back (to protect them) and its tail stiff. The tail is easy to read, so keep an eye on it when two rabbits meet each other for the first time.

Most rabbits have ears that are upright, but of course you might have a beautiful lop-eared rabbit. Reading the body language of a lop-eared rabbit can be difficult, as their ears move only slightly. Basically, lop-eared rabbits will signal relaxation by letting their ears hang close to the body. A nervous or aggressive lop-eared rabbit will pull back its ears a little bit. Just like we find it difficult to interpret the body language of a lop-eared rabbit, we can only assume that other rabbits find it a challenge too. So, in theory it might be more difficult to bond lop-eared rabbits.

Curious rabbit

Rabbit about to attack

Before You Get Started

We know that rabbits are social animals, so why is it sometimes so difficult to bond them? Sometimes their personalities just do not match, but most often it is because we are using the wrong approaches to bond them. Maybe we have put the rabbits in situations that are stressful for them. All too many rabbit owners have tried putting two rabbits that do not know each other into a cage. Because the rabbits have fought, the rabbit owner has come to the conclusion that rabbits are not social animals or that at least that these particular rabbits are not. The truth is that simply placing two rabbits together in a small space and expecting them to live happily ever after cannot be described as an actual attempt at bonding rabbits.

Do your groundwork
What rabbit owners most often do wrong is to simply put the two rabbits in front of each other and expect a friendship to arise straightaway. This can certainly happen, but in most cases, it does not. It is important to remember that rabbits have some very basic social rules for behavior and interaction, just like we humans have. We call it rabbit etiquette.

Two rabbits that meet each other for the first time under natural conditions will size each other up by first ignoring each other — from a distance. This gives them the opportunity to find out who the other one is from their scent and behaviour and finally determine whether the other rabbit is friendly or not. Once the rabbits feel confident enough to approach each other, it will happen very slowly — and always from the side. Slowly, they move towards each other, often interrupted by pauses to groom themselves and forage. They are careful not to show a keen interest in each other. To the outsider, they seem unaware of each other - in reality, they are giving each other friendly signals, while the distance at the same time provides them with the opportunity to immediately withdraw if the situation requires it.

Some rabbit owners find it difficult waiting out this slow process. They get frustrated because the two rabbits do not seem interested in each other. They try to force the rabbits physically closer together, putting the rabbits in a very uncomfortable situation — furthermore it is bad rabbit etiquette. Now there is a risk that things will go very wrong. If the rabbits are forced to be close together, possibly even on the old rabbit's territory, it will be very difficult to avoid a conflict between the rabbits. Because of the lack of space, the new rabbit cannot withdraw as rabbit etiquette dictates. The result is an open invitation to fight. The old rabbit will understandably try to chase away the — very provocative — newcomer. If there is not enough space to display ritualized aggression (which rabbits use in order not to harm each other) and no way to escape the situation, the two rabbits are caught in a very unpleasant situation. The newcomer cannot physically withdraw from the situation, and the old rabbit can only interpret it in one way: This new rabbit wants to fight! And so the fighting begins, even if neither rabbit really wanted it.

That is why it is so important to know your rabbit's temperament before you begin the bonding process, and also to have some basic knowledge of rabbit behavior.

In addition, you must have enough space for two or more rabbits. Rabbits are active animals and need lots of room to thrive. It is always best to let your rabbits live a cage-free life, or at least give them a large fenced area to run around in. You will need a minimum of 15 square meters (12 square feet) for two rabbits.

How age and sex affect bonding

It is easiest to bond two rabbits of the opposite sex. That does not mean that friendship is impossible between two males or two females though — only that it may require more work. If you have no experience in bonding rabbits, it is better to try to bond one male and one female rabbit. A male and female rabbit will have a natural attraction between each other, which means that this type of bonding is often very easy.

The younger the rabbits are, the easier it will be to bond them. Two young sexually mature male rabbits of the same age can be a challenge though. A better combination would be one older and one younger male rabbit, or just two older male rabbits. The same applies for females. Although many find that females are less friendly than males, it is actually easier to bond two females than two males.

Neutering

For a successful bonding both rabbits need to be neutered. No exceptions. Female rabbits can be spayed as soon as they are four months old. With male rabbits, you often have to wait until the testicles descend, although some vets can easily neuter the males at just 10-12 weeks old. It all depends on your vet. Neutering gets rid of any territorial behavior related to hormones. When a rabbit is neutered, its body stops producing fertility hormones. That means territorial behavior connected with defending a mate or a nest in the warren will be minimized, because the rabbit is no longer in a nonstop mating season.

Whatever sex you want to bond, things will go much more smoothly when your rabbits are neutered. There are many stories of intact female rabbits that live together peacefully, and even stories about intact male rabbits, but this cannot be recommended. As a rule of thumb, rabbits of the same sex should have been neutered for at least 6 weeks before you begin the bonding process in order to avoid any territorial conflicts. In the end though, it all comes down to the personality of your rabbits. Evaluate the situation based on their behavior. For rabbits of the opposite sex, it can be an advantage to bond them right after they are neutered. This is particularly true if you are introducing a new female rabbit to your male rabbit. Hormones here will be a big help — sometimes the bonding process can take just a few minutes! Make sure though that the female has enough space to withdraw from the male rabbit if he is too eager. Not only is she recovering from surgery and need to heal, but the male rabbit's constant attention can also be too stressful for her. If you get the feeling that the female rabbit needs rest, wait a bit longer before you introduce them.

If you have two young rabbits that have been living happily together before the neuter, there is no reason to keep them apart afterwards for the hormones to settle (unless they need to be separated to heal properly). They are already bonded, even if you did not do anything to make that happen. If the two friends suddenly fall out, it can sometimes be necessary to separate them though and keep one of them in a run in their shared space, until the hormone levels have decreased.

Unacceptable behavior

Ideally, aggressive behavior or mounting should not be observed during bonding, and in most cases you will not see any of it. It does happen, however, so it is important to know in advance why it happens and how you should react.

Aggression

Are some rabbits unable to get along with other rabbits? Yes, occasionally a rabbit cannot "speak rabbit" and does not get along with other rabbits. Fortunately, this is rare. In most cases when a rabbit does not get along with other rabbits, it is because the rabbit just does not fit in well with this particular group. There is a chance that the unsociable rabbit becomes friendly and relaxed if placed in a different group with a strong, dominant rabbit. Being introduced to such a group will make the rabbit more relaxed, because the hierarchy is already established and solid. Of course, the rabbit needs to accept its new rank as subordinate and not challenge the dominant rabbit in the group for it to work.

Aggressive behavior in a rabbit almost always has an explanation. Most often, it is a sign of stress or timidity/anxiety. The rabbit will use attack as its best form of defense. If a rabbit shows signs of aggression during bonding or towards its rabbit friends, it is very important to always find the cause to why it is not happy. Do not simply write the rabbit off as aggressive or unsocial. An aggressive rabbit is very often a misunderstood rabbit. Rabbits are not aggressive by nature, but they are territorial, and they have sharp teeth and claws they use to defend themselves when they feel threatened. Poor rabbit communication skills, bad experiences with other rabbits, wrong bonding techniques or just insecurities in the rabbit can make for a rabbit that is afraid of other rabbits or easy to stress during the bonding process. This makes it look hostile and aggressive to us. In reality, it is simply scared and it needs you to be a better help during the bonding process. If you have a rabbit that acts aggressively during bonding, look more closely at what is happening and see if there is something you can do to make your rabbit feel safer. When does your rabbit show signs of aggression? What happens right before that? Maybe you have just carried the rabbit to a neutral place to begin the bonding process. Being picked up is unpleasant and scary for most rabbits. If your rabbit is a little nervous in the first place, being picked up and carried somewhere else can be a bad start to the bonding process. The rabbit's insecurity may also have something to do with being in unknown territory, or maybe it is simply just a timid rabbit.

As mentioned earlier, rabbits use ritualized aggression as a way to solve conflicts without hurting each other. It is a display in which they run towards each other, jump, chase each other, bite each other's fur, dig, lift their tails, and spray each other with urine. This ritualized aggression is essentially a harmless form of aggression that is intended to intimidate the other rabbit, so it backs off. During these displays, submissive behavior is usually seen on the part of one of the rabbits, or it withdraws to make the conflict stop. For many rabbit owners, it can be difficult to see the difference between ritualized aggression and an actual fight. That of course makes it difficult to know how to react. When you bond two neutered rabbits of the opposite sex, these situations are very unusual. But if you have many rabbits of the same sex, you may see this type of behavior, so be careful to choose the appropriate approach to bonding your rabbits, so you avoid a real fight.

Mounting

Mounting, or humping, another rabbit is not an attempt to dominate. Rabbits do not use sexual positions to establish a hierarchy or show their rank within a group. The truth is mounting is caused by stress. It is a sign that the rabbit is nervous or anxious. Mounting is a way to release stress from the body, but it should always be stopped. It is unpleasant for the rabbit that is mounted, and for the rabbit doing the mounting, it is a clear sign that the situation is too much to handle. Until some years ago, when it was still believed that it was an attempt to establish a hierarchy, many rabbit owners said that you should simply let the rabbits mount each other, so they could "work it out together." Since mounting is not a case of dominance or "working it out", you should always stop it. If the mounting continues, stop the bonding sessions and try to figure out another way to approach the situation, so you do not stress the rabbit too much. Consider giving the rabbit a stuffed animal to mount and relieve its stress.

Are you trying to bond a male and female and mounting occurs, it is most often because one or both has been neutered shortly before the bonding process. It can still be a case of stress, but it may also be because the male rabbit can smell a lovely female rabbit and love is in the air. Most male and female rabbits work this out on their own if there is enough space for the female rabbit to get away from the overeager male rabbit. If she cannot get away from him, she may bite him. You want to avoid this from happening.

When are they bonded?
Some rabbit owners say that rabbits are only fully bonded when they groom each other. If that is the case, you may have to wait quite a while. Instead of using grooming as a guideline, look at the rabbits instead. Are they relaxed? Do they eat and sleep close to each other? Good. They are bonded. There is, unfortunately, no set rule for how long it takes to bond rabbits. Some rabbits are each other's best friends after half an hour, while for others it may take several weeks. The vast majority of rabbits are bonded within two or three weeks.

If your rabbits are not free-range, but you need them to be in a run when you are out, you have to use as much time to bond them in the run as it took to bond them in the first place in a neutral or big area. Allow for plenty of time for the bonding process if this is the case.

Very rarely, it will it take several months to bond rabbits. If you are unlucky enough to be in this situation, it is time to consider if this is the right match and if it is fair to continue to put them under this stress.

I cannot emphasize enough that until the rabbits have spent several days in a row without problems, they should not be left together without supervision.

Let the Bonding Begin

We influence the bonding process with our interferences (or lack of). Some rabbit owners are better at reading the body language than others, and we all bring in our own personality and experience to the bonding process. What works for one rabbit owner does not work for another. Every bonding process is unique because we are different, the situation is different, and the rabbits are different. That actually makes it impossible to make a guide that fits every situation, but the techniques described here will certainly help you.

You will find three approaches to bonding. Choose the one that best fits you and your rabbits. You can even combine them.

The stress-free bonding
Level of difficulty: 🐇 🐇 🐇 🐇
Stress level: 🐇 🐇 🐇 🐇
Requirements: A run.
Best suited for: All rabbits. This is the best approach for territorial or nervous rabbits, as well as new rabbit owners.

This technique is the absolute least stressful — for both the rabbit owner and the rabbits. To sum it up, you do no actual work, but let the rabbits get used to each other through the bars of a run. This approach can be combined with "The classic bonding" or stand on its own. It works particularly well with territorial rabbits, even though you will be letting a strange rabbit move into the territory. Because of the bars between them and because they themselves choose when to interact, they are not as stressed about the other rabbit as they would otherwise be. If your rabbits have just been neutered, this is the best approach, since you can begin to bond them right away without waiting several weeks.

How to do it
The new rabbit is placed in a run in the living area, or wherever your old rabbit likes to be. You can certainly place the run in an area, where your rabbit rarely comes, but then the bonding process can take a long time, so it is not recommended. Make sure that the space between the bars does not make it possible for one of the rabbits to squeeze through. Also make sure the rabbit cannot escape the run. The run should ideally be about two

square meters (21 square feet). As a minimum, it should have a litter box and a cardboard box where the rabbit can spend time. The cardboard box should have two holes. Put food close to the bars, so the rabbits can eat in the vicinity of each other. The litter box and the cardboard box should be placed so that there is space around them. Otherwise, there is a risk that the new rabbit can get stuck between the bars and the box and not be able to get away quickly enough if your old rabbit comes running to bite. The same considerations apply to the run itself. It should either be placed so it is right up against the wall or with so much space between the wall and the run that the old rabbit can pass by easily. To prevent the rabbits from jumping in or out of the run, you can put a net or something similar on top.

It is important that both rabbits can choose whether they want contact and interaction with each other or not. The old rabbit should be able to go into another area of the house or at least move out of eyesight if it does not want to be in contact with the new rabbit, and the new rabbit should be able to go in his box or withdraw to the back of the run without the old rabbit coming close. Make sure both rabbits have tasty treats near the bars, so they associate each other with something good and come close to each other. But do not force them.

Now the waiting game begins. You simply just wait for the rabbits to get used to each other and begin to bond. In the beginning, you will probably see a great deal of ritualized aggression or actual attempts to fight. If they begin to bite each other, put up some kind of finely woven netting, so they can still see each other but cannot harm each other. As soon as they relax in each other's company and are no longer biting through the bars, demonstratively digging, running with raised tails along the run or marking their territory in any other way, you can let them meet each other without the bars between them. It usually takes two to three weeks before this happens, but it varies. The rabbits should be friendly towards each other (or basically not showing any signs of ritualized aggression) for several days in a row before you can move on to the next part of the bonding process.

Open the run early in the morning on a day when you have time to sit with them all day as well as the day after. Make sure the rabbits have plenty of space when the run is removed, and that there are pellets and greens distributed around the floor. Remove the litter boxes, cardboard boxes and other things the rabbits might claim as their territory. You want to set a happy and relaxed atmosphere. You can put those things back again a little bit at a time when you can see that the rabbits are relaxed and that the objects are not creating problems. Speak quietly and calmly to the rabbits. Pet them and create a pleasant atmosphere. If there is no sign of territorial behavior, let them be together for the rest of the day, but put the new rabbit in the run for the night before you leave them. Let them meet again the next day and remain nearby. You will probably be able to let them be together without problems after two days with supervision, but this can vary.

If any biting or chasing occurs, you may have opened up the run too quickly. Put the rabbit back in the run and wait two more weeks. You can also choose to combine this approach with "The classic bonding" approach. If you combine the two, the first time the rabbits meet outside the run, it should be on neutral ground.

The classic bonding
Level of difficulty: 🐰 🐰 🐇 🐇
Stress level: 🐰 🐰 🐇 🐇
Requirements: Neutral area.
Best suited for: All rabbits, except for nervous or insecure rabbits.

"The classic bonding" approach is probably the most popular one for many rabbit owners - simply because this is the one most rabbit owners know about. To sum it up, you introduce the rabbits in a neutral area. By letting them get to know each other in a neutral area, you do not put the rabbits in a situation where they need to defend their territory. In a neutral area, they will be less territorial. This approach has some significant advantages, but also disadvantages. Removed from their safe surroundings, the rabbits will feel insecure and at the same time, you are forcing two strange rabbits together in a confined space. This approach is as a result more stressful for the rabbits (and you) than "The stress-free bonding" approach, and there is a risk that the rabbits will begin to fight if you have not given them enough space, or if they feel anxious. For this approach to work, you need to be good at interpreting their body language. "The classic bonding" approach also requires that you can devote yourself to the bonding process and to create a quiet, calm atmosphere. It is better to put aside a few consecutive full days for this bonding process than to use 30 minutes a day for a longer period of time.

If you choose to bond your rabbits with this approach on a neutral area, your role is very important. It is your job to create a positive atmosphere, to calm an anxious rabbit and stop any inappropriate behavior — without disturbing the bonding process.

If you have two young rabbits or a male and a female rabbit that you would like to bond, this is the quickest and easiest way to bond them. Keep in mind, however, that this can be a slightly stressful technique that is not well suited to nervous rabbits.

How to do it

Try to find a place in your home where your rabbit has never been before. It should be an entirely neutral area for both rabbits. Since many rabbit owners have free-range rabbits, it can be hard to find an entirely neutral area, but think creatively. It can be the bathroom, the basement, the shed or even the dining table. Some rabbit owners use the bathtub, but there is very little room in the bathtub, so if you choose such a small area, be sure that both rabbits have a laid-back temperament. This approach will probably involve a lot of marking with excrement and urine, so I do suggest that you do not do this on a bed.

Since the whole idea behind this approach is to use neutral areas to avoid territorial behavior, you cannot have anything in the neutral area that the rabbits can claim as their territory. Do not put out the litter box, cardboard boxes, etc. If you have a nervous rabbit, it can be necessary though to give it a litter box where it can go to feel safe, but in that case, it is important that you make sure neither one of the rabbits begins to claim the litter box as territory. And you should keep the other rabbit away, if the nervous rabbit gets into its box. Do not put food or treats in bowls in the area, but distribute it evenly on the floor. Lots of food is always good when bonding. It is not possible to be aggressive or alert while eating. Eating has a calming effect on the rabbit. While the rabbit eats and is calm, it also sends friendly, calming signals to the other rabbit. The more they eat, the better!

Now place the rabbits in the neutral area and let them greet each other in their own pace. It can be a good idea to keep a hand on them at all times by petting them a lot, so you can get a sense of whether they are relaxed or tense. That way you can take action before anything happens. If you feel one of the rabbits is tightening its muscles and maybe moving its head in the direction of the other, put a soft hand over its head, so your thumb moves up and down over the nose tip and your other fingers caress it around the eye. This way you can hold the rabbit back while you calm it. If you notice one of the rabbits is on guard, put a soft hand loosely on its back, so you can quickly hold it back if necessary. If you are afraid of being bitten, find a round splatter guard (to put on a frying pan) and quickly place it between the rabbits if necessary.

Do not force the rabbits close together. It is fine if they just keep to themselves for the first few days, remaining at opposite ends of the area and ignoring each other. This is entirely positive.

When you use this technique, it is important that you keep an eye on the rabbits' body language (see page 8) so you can avoid any fights. If they come close to each other, pet them even more, speak quietly and tell them that you need them to be friends.

This approach requires a sharp eye and patience on your part. Your job is to ensure the rabbits meet each other in a friendly matter while you control what happens. Do not interfere if it is not necessary, and do not confuse ritualized aggression with an actual intention to hurt each other. It can be tempting to go in and meddle with the process, but you will cause problems rather than helping to solve them. The rabbits must never hurt each other, although when you bond them in a small area, you may see that they chase each other and bite each other's fur. This is acceptable up to a point in the bonding process, but should be avoided. Your job is to make sure that no actual fight happens by keeping an eye on their body language, making sure they are busy with their tasty treats and that there is a good atmosphere. If they start to fight, the bonding process must be stopped right away. In that case, it is better that you use "The stress-free bonding" approach instead.

When you feel it is going well between the rabbits in the neutral area and that they can eat and relax quite close to each other, it is time to bond them in the area where they will live together in the future. It is important that you do not skip this part of the bonding process. You actually need to start all over from the beginning once again and use the exact same techniques you used in the neutral area. In other words, spread the treats across the floor, remove the litter box, cardboard boxes, etc. so there is nothing that can be claimed as a territory and place your hands on the rabbits.

Little by little, you can start to put things back as their friendship strengthens. Make sure you also clean everything thoroughly and maybe even move the furniture around before you begin the bonding process if this is where your old rabbit usually resides. That helps make the territory a bit less well established. Put aside plenty of time for the last part of the bonding process, particularly if your rabbits are not free roaming. The smaller the space, the longer you have to wait before they can share the space without supervision.

The stress bonding
Level of difficulty: 🐇 🐇 🐇 🐇
Stress: 🐇 🐇 🐇 🐇
Requirements: Two people, one car.
Best-suited for: Same-sex rabbits that cannot get along.

"The stress bonding" approach is an unusual approach, because it is without any consideration to the well-being of the rabbits. It is very stressful for them — hence the name. This approach can be used when the bonding approaches have gone all wrong and all the other solutions you have tried have failed. This approach is not only unpleasant for the rabbits, but it also breaks the rabbit etiquette rules. That is why it should be used only when you have tried in vain more rabbit-friendly approaches.

Because the approach is so stressful, there is a risk that the method can backfire. The rabbits may associate the uncomfortable experience with each other and never become friends, or the bonding process may be further delayed. So why is it mentioned in this book at all? Because some rabbit owners use this approach as a means to begin the bonding, I find it important to explain the approach. It may also be useful for some rabbit owners who have been trying for a long time without achieving a successful bonding. It is important to emphasize that you should only use this approach once you have already tried and failed with everything else.

How to do it
Place the two rabbits in an open pet carrier or laundry basket and put them in the back seat of a car. Get someone to drive the car while you sit with the rabbits so you can make sure they do not fight. The point of the car trip is that the sound of the motor and the shaking of the car will scare

the rabbits so much that they will huddle together and seek comfort in each other. Hopefully afterwards they will associate each other with the feeling of comfort and a friendship will blossom. After a 10-15 minute drive, put the rabbits in a neutral area and begin "The classic bonding" approach.
If the rabbits begin to fight as soon as they get out of the car, do not let them meet on neutral ground, but take a car trip every day for two weeks. Whenever the rabbits are not in the car or in the neutral area, they should be entirely apart from each other and not able see each other.

Some rabbit owners put the rabbits on top of a tumble drier or a washing machine on centrifuge setting instead of a car. It is not as effective as a car trip, but if you do not have a car it will suffice. Two rabbits that really want to fight are going to fight whether they are placed on top of a tumble dryer or in a car. That is why this technique requires two people to be present.

The approach is very stressful, so it is important that you constantly watch the rabbits to see how they are doing. Consider carefully if it is really worth it to put them through this. Nervous rabbits in particular will suffer a great deal during this form of bonding process.

Bonding multiple rabbits
Level of difficulty: 🐰🐰🐰🐰
Stress level: 🐰🐰🐰🐰
Requirements: A run for each new rabbit, a neutral area.
Best suited for: All rabbits.

Most rabbit owners with several rabbits would like them all to live together. How should you approach the bonding process if you have three or four rabbits that you would like to live together?
The easiest is to use "The stress-free bonding" approach in the case of a single rabbit moving in with an existing group. "The stress-free bonding" approach can be combined with "The classic bonding" approach, where you let the rabbits after a while meet each other one-on-one on neutral ground. This entirely depends on the temperament of you and your rabbits. If you have several new rabbits you need to bond, it is a good idea to use "The classic bonding" approach, so you bond them one at a time in pairs.

How to do it

Let the new rabbit move into the run on the other rabbits' territory. When you no longer see any form of digging, running up and down along the run, raised tails, etc., you can begin "The classic bonding" approach. The new rabbit should continue to live in the run until all they are all bonded.

Let the dominant rabbit (probably your oldest male or female) be the first to meet the new rabbit in a neutral area. The dominant rabbit's job is to stop conflicts within the group and you will often see this rabbit interfere if there is any commotion in the group, so it is a good idea to start here. If problems arise between the new rabbit and some of the other rabbits in the group later in the bonding process, you have the dominant rabbit to serve as a peacemaker. Once the dominant rabbit and your new rabbit get along well together, it is time to introduce your new rabbit to one of the other rabbits in a neutral area, just the two of them. Continue this way.

Once your new rabbit has met and become friends with each individual rabbit, it is time to increase the number of rabbits in the neutral area. Start over again with the dominant rabbit, your new rabbit and the rabbit that was most welcoming and friendly to the newcomer. When all is well between the three of them, you can let another one of the rabbits take part in the bonding process in the neutral area.

When you feel that it is going well between the rabbits in the neutral area, it is time for them to meet each other on their territory. You now have to start all over again. Repeat what you did in the neutral area. It rarely takes as much time to get the rabbits to get along on the old territory, when they have first come to know each other in the neutral area, but it is an important part of the bonding process. Of course, you need to keep the other rabbits away, as you introduce the rabbits one by one in their living area.

When Nothing Goes as Planned...

Sometimes it can be impossible for even the most experienced rabbit owner to make two rabbits like each other. No matter what approach you use, the rabbits fight. This is usually seen when trying to bond two young male rabbits of the same age.

If the bonding process affects the rabbits to the point that they are clearly stressed (if they try to bite you or start losing weight) then it is time to stop, because they are no longer happy. It can be very difficult to give up. It might mean you have to say goodbye to a rabbit you are fond of. But remember that there are many good homes for rabbits out there — places where your rabbit will be happier and can find a rabbit friend with whom it can have a peaceful life. It is our obligation to our four-legged friends to make sure that they live the best life possible. Sometimes that is not living with us.

Luckily most attempts at bonding rabbits do succeed sooner or later. So, before you completely throw in the towel, consider separating the rabbits entirely for a period of at least three weeks. They should not see or smell each other during this period. Give them something calming. If they have been tense and stressed over a long period of time, they need help to calm down again. The more relaxed they are when the bonding process begins again, and the more they have put the bad encounters behind them, the easier it will be to bond them. You can find a number of calming products for rabbits — the most popular ones are Pet Remedy, Bach's Rescue Remedy and Chamomilla, which is a homeopathic remedy. These remedies can also be used before you even begin the bonding in the first place. Do also try rabbit massages to relieve the tension and stress. There are many great books on the subject.

Once the rabbits are looking much more relaxed and it has been a couple of weeks since the last bonding session, start all over from the beginning by using "The stress-free bonding" approach, while you continue to give them the calming remedies. Keep an eye on their body language. The body language will tell you when they are ready to move on to the next step.

If the bonding process is not in a complete deadlock but the sessions are just not progressing as easily as you hoped, consider carefully if you might be doing something wrong. Have you stressed the rabbits too much? Are you reading their body language incorrectly? Is your rabbit not actually aggressive, just stressed and nervous? Is the space too small? Have you tried to bond your rabbits too quickly? Have you removed everything your rabbits could claim as their territory? Has something happened during the bonding process that could have affected the rabbits, such as changes in your home or family? Look closely at your rabbits and their behavior based on what you have learned about rabbits in this book and see if you can change the bonding process so it becomes less stressful for them. It could be you are influencing the bonding process in a negative fashion if you feel stressed yourself, so perhaps there is someone in your circle of friends who can help by taking over the bonding process for you.

Bonding with Your Rabbit

We all want a rabbit that loves us and wants to cuddle, and that is why the bonding process between you and your rabbit is just as important.

Most rabbits that move into a new home will be a bit nervous and not overly eager to be petted. Do not worry. This can all change within the next two weeks or months. While some rabbits just love everyone they meet, other rabbits take a bit of time before they ease up and want to be petted. If you have such a rabbit, these tips will help you.

- Sleep with an old t-shirt for a few nights and then place it in the rabbit's sleeping area, so that it gets used to your smell.

- Give your rabbit a treat every time you sit down near it. Yes, that is probably a lot of treats, but remember this is just for a period (and try to give healthy treats). Once your rabbit feels confident coming to you for treats, begin to say its name before giving the treat. Slowly decrease the space between you and the rabbit and pet it while giving the treat. In the beginning you may only get to touch your rabbit for a second before it runs off, but keep it up. Continue several times a day for at least a month or two.

- Lie down on the floor and ignore the rabbit. The more you ignore it, the better. Read a book, watch TV. Let the rabbit sniff and nip as much as it wants. Just do not look at it. This gives the most timid rabbits the confidence to get closer to you and get to know you that way.

Finally, it should not be necessary to point this out, yet too many rabbit owners seem to forget: do not lift your rabbit. If you want your rabbit to sit on your lap and be petted, sit on the floor and slowly teach your rabbit to jump into your lap by giving it treats, but never force it. The more you lift your rabbit, the more cautious it might become of you. Whatever deep friendship you were hoping for, cannot develop if the rabbit is afraid of you. So, let the friendship with your rabbit grow on its terms, never yours.

Frequently Asked Questions

Through the years I have helped many rabbit owners before, during and even after the bonding process. They mostly ask the same questions. To help you with your bonding process I have listed the most frequently asked questions here as well as answers to them, which might be of help to you.

? I have a 2-year old rabbit. He has always been good at using his litter box, and we have only ever had a few accidents. Last month I got him a female friend to keep him company. They bonded very quickly and they are good friends. Unfortunately, my boy is no longer litter trained. He poops everywhere now. What happened and what can I do?

! Unfortunately, it happens quite often that an otherwise perfectly litter trained rabbit begins to mark when a new rabbit moves in. Even if they are best friends. It begins out of nowhere and usually the problem resolves just as quickly by itself. Sometimes it takes three weeks, sometimes maybe two months. There is no explanation other than your rabbit has become more aware of its territory. The best thing you can do is to wash the floor thoroughly each day, wash the walls and if possible also move things around a bit. You need to get rid of any scent markings in your home. See if your rabbit perhaps needs more cardboard boxes to make him feel more secure, and while you are washing everything down in their living area, it might be a good idea to try not to change the litter box too often during this period. It might comfort your rabbit if the toilet has his scent (of course, don't let it get too dirty).

? We are very new to the world of bunnies. Our daughter got her first bunny about a month ago, and I must admit that I love it. I am thinking of getting more bunnies now. I really want them all bonded in a big enclosure in the garden. Will this work? What combination of sexes do you suggest? Do they all need to be neutered? What do I do if they cannot get along?

! Rabbits are wonderful animals, so I understand why you want to fill up your house and garden with rabbits. However, before you do so, do take a few deep breaths. While a multiple rabbit household is definitely great fun, it does require space and some rabbit knowledge. The more rabbits, you want, the more space you need to provide them. Try to start out with just two rabbits, so you get the hang of it. Once this is working out for you, then you can consider adding another rabbit to the family. But first start out with a rabbit of the opposite sex of what you have today. They should both be neutered. It is very rare that two neutered rabbits of the opposite sex do not get along, so do not worry. If you decide to add a third rabbit, a neutered female might be best, but it depends on the personality of your rabbits. If your male is very docile and relaxed, then go for another male.

? When is it okay to interfere when I am bonding my rabbits? I know that any time we interrupt or stop their communication during a bonding session, they have to start all over again. But when is it okay then?

! There is a difference in disrupting the communication between the rabbits and to help them move in the right direction. See yourself as the alpha rabbit, the dominant rabbit. It's your job to make sure that there is a relaxed atmosphere, and no biting takes place at any time. Your job is to calm the anxious, stressed or tense rabbit with your voice and by petting it. You have to foresee what happens next by reading their body language and to prevent negative behavior. You have to make sure that there is plenty of treats on the floor all over the place and that they can withdraw from the situation, if they need to. If you do your job right, then you won't have to interfere or disrupt the communication. Your job is basically to avoid having to interfere, because then your have skipped some important steps in the bonding process.

? I am thinking of getting two rabbits. Do I need to buy two of everything then? Two litter boxes, food bowls etc.?

! It can be a great idea to give each rabbit its own litter box to begin with. They may still only use the same litter box, but to avoid any accidents outside the litter box, it is better to give them more options. If you only have one litter box, one of them might not feel comfortable using it in the beginning and will poop everywhere else. Also, do give each of them their own cardboard box, treat ball/food dispenser etc.

? I want to begin bonding my two rabbits on neutral territory, but I'm afraid they will fight. I have never tried bonding rabbits before. What do I do if they start to fight?

! If you choose "The classic bonding" approach and put two new rabbits together in a neutral area you do run the risk that they will show ritualized aggression — or in the worst case if they do not have enough space for it, actually fight. The best you can do is to have a splatter guard ready. That way you can — without risk being bitten — quickly stop the fight. If you are afraid that they will fight though, you should not choose this bonding approach to begin with. You should choose "The stress-free bonding" approach.

? I have a really sweet and cuddly bunny. He loves to give me kisses and hang out with me on the couch. I have read that rabbits should have a companion, but if I get him a bunny wife, will he be less interested in me?

! Your rabbit will still enjoy being petted as much as he did before. His need for cuddles and affection will still be the same. And he will also be the same as before. However, it is no secret that rabbits do prefer the company of other rabbits to the company of humans. So, if he has to choose between you and his new wife, he will choose her. But that's not bad. It just means that you have made him happy by giving him a friend. And do remember that now you may just have two rabbits to kiss and cuddle instead of one.

? My two rabbits have been good friends for two years. They had a fight last night, because I woke up and found fur tufts on the floor. Do I need to separate them? Should I re-bond them?

! Sometimes even the best of friends have a disagreement — it happens to humans and to rabbits. It does not necessarily mean that you rabbits are no longer friends. If it happens again then try to find out what triggers the fight. Do they feel trapped in a small cage or run at night? Has something changed in your house? Did you or your neighbor get a dog? Stressed rabbits are more likely to fall out over the smallest things. The same applies for rabbits that are ill or in pain. Try to observe your rabbits and their environment to find the cause. If it only happens once in a while and they are happy again the next day, then don't worry. As long as they are not confined in a small space. If the fighting continues, then you should definitely have them checked by a vet and then begin bonding all over again.

? Is it impossible to bond two does that are not spayed? I have just rescued two does from an awful place. We have no vets nearby who want to spay them. They are not used to living together.

! It is not recommended, and I would not do it myself, but I do know of quite a few rabbit owners who have intact does living happily together. If they are not already bonded and they are used to living together, you must prepare yourself for a bonding process that can take many months. Also, you need plenty of space. Let them live side by side for a few months ("The stress-free bonding") and then let them meet on neutral ground. Your neutral space has to be a very large area (minimum 40 m^2/ 430 square feet). You need to apply the techniques from "The classic bonding" approach as well as "The stress-free bonding" approach and combine them. Plenty of space and patience is what is needed for this. If you do not have enough space, maybe you should consider not bonding them. The best solution is of course to find a vet further away who will spay them.

? We really need help bonding four rabbits. We have a large backyard and here we have a 6 m² run (64 square feet). This is their main living area. The run has access to an even bigger enclosure of 22 m² (236 square feet), which they will have access to when we are home. We have a new female rabbit, a new male, and then we have our old bonded pair. All of them are neutered. At the moment they are all living inside the house. Today we tried to bond them in a neutral area that is 20 m² (215 square feet). We let them all out at once. It ended in fights. The two females were very aggressive, and our old female even attacked us. We have separated them now, but they are all very tense. We hope for a happy ending, but the bonding went so horribly wrong today that we are afraid to try again.

! What a stressful event for both you and the rabbits. It's quite a risky and stressful approach to bonding you chose. That's one thing. But the area you want the 4 rabbits to live in is much too small. You expect 4 rabbits to live on 6 m² most of the time? That's not even enough for one rabbit. Of course you have the extra space, but that is only for a few hours a day. You need to re-evaluate the situation, before you proceed with the bonding, because it will be too stressful for the rabbits to live together in such a small space. In regard to the bonding it's quite a chaotic approach. What ages are the rabbits? If the two of the same sex are the same age, you might have a challenge ahead of you. Trying to bond them all at once is very stressful for them — and you. You need to bond them one by one. It will take time to bond 4 new rabbits, and you need lots of patience. Usually it is better to bond the dominant rabbit with the newcomer first and take it from there, but in this case, you probably need some reassurance first and foremost and some positive bonding practice, so begin with the two most docile rabbits. Once they are bonded, take the most docile rabbit again and bond it with another rabbit. Bond only two rabbits at a time. When all four rabbits have been bonded in all combinations, you are ready to begin bonding them 3 at a time in the different possible combinations.

? We got 2 cute females 3 weeks ago. They are now 11-12 weeks old. Until now they have shared a cage in our living room. We didn't want to let them out, because we didn't want to stress them too much by introducing them to a big new area at once. The other day we noticed that the little black one chased and bit the other one. She was also humping her We have bought another cage, so they are separated now and live in separate rooms. This morning we let them out together in the living room, but the little black one attacked its sister straight away. Why does she do that? And what can we do? Everything was fine until the other day.

! It's unfortunate that they are fighting, but the positive thing is that you reacted quickly and separated them. Although they are still very young, the small cage has probably not been very good for them. Rabbits need plenty of space not to stress, and when they are stressed or just cannot get away from each other, they do get more irritable which can lead to fights. Probably the black one is starting to sexually mature, which is a trigger. I assume that you are 100% sure of the sex? Since they keep fighting, it is better to keep them separated until they have been neutered and then wait for them to calm down. However, let them have close contact until you can let them out together. Buy two runs and place them side by side. They can still enjoy each other's company, communicate and develop their friendship — they just cannot fight. Hopefully, the neuter will help, and these tiffs are only due to limited space and sexual maturity.

? My boyfriend and I have a male rabbit. He is 3 years old and neutered. We decided to get him a friend and bought a sweet little girl. She was 3 months old when we bonded them. They liked each other quite quickly and groomed each other all the time and seemed almost glued to each other. After 2 months, suddenly our girl began to nip him. We had her spayed and kept them separated. We have tried everything, but she keeps biting him and seems to want to fight with him. We have separated them and keep them in two cages close to each other. We swap litter boxes and teddy bears every day. It doesn't seem to help. What can we do?

Sometimes it can take quite a while before the effects of the neuter really kicks in and the hormonal level goes down, especially if she was undergoing a false pregnancy, also known as pseudopregnancy, when the spaying took place. It sounds like you have done everything else right. Unfortunately you need to start all over with the bonding. It would be better if they were not kept in cages, but in runs, as runs are bigger. Also, you only need one run, so one has free access to the living room and the other is kept in the run (preferably the female should be in the run). That way they can choose when to interact. Place their food close to each other, so they will eat near each other. It calms them down. Do not swap litter boxes and teddy bears etc. It's actually more stressful for them. They need to feel calm and secure in their own area. And don't worry; they can still smell each other just fine. Do this for 2-3 weeks and then let the female out — with supervision, lots of treats and no litter boxes etc. to fight about. This is "The stress-free bonding" approach.

References

Comfortable Quarters for Laboratory Animals by Animal Welfare Institute, 2015.

Behavior of Exotic Pets by Valarie V. Tynes, 2010.

Social behaviour of an experimental colony of wild rabbits, Oryctolagus cuniculus (L.) III. Second breeding season by R Mykytowycz, 1960.

Development of hierarchy and rank effects in weaned growing rabbits (Oryctolagus Cuniculus) by H. Vervaecke H. et. al., 2003.

Warren Use in Open and Covered Habitats: the importance of predation for the European rabbit (Oryctolagus cuniculus) By Laura Smith, 2003.

Refinements in rabbit husbandry: Second report of the BVAAWF/FRAME/RSPCA/UFAW by D B Morton et al., 1993.

Behavioral styles in European rabbits: Social interactions and responses to experimental stressors by Heiko G. Rödel et al., 2006.

Social rank, fecundity and lifetime reproductive success in wild European rabbits (Oryctolagus cuniculus) by Dietrich von Holst et al., 2001.

Textbook of rabbit medicine by Frances Harcourt-Brown, 2002.

The behaviour of individually housed growing rabbits and influence of gnawing sticks as environmental enrichment on daily rhythm of behavioral patterns duration by Dušanka Jordan et al., 2010.

The effects of group housing on the research use of the laboratory rabbit by Mark Whary et al., 1993.

Social Structure and Stress in the Rabbit Warren by R.M. Lockley, 1961.

The Private Life of Rabbits by R.M. Lockley, 1954.

Further reading

Would you like to learn more about rabbits as pets the following books are recommended.

Understanding Your Rabbits' Habits by Tamsin Stone.

House Rabbit Handbook: How to Live with an Urban Rabbit by Marinell Harriman.

Why Does My rabbit...? by Anne McBride.

Rabbit Language or Are You Going to Eat That? by Carolyn R. Crampton.

Printed in Great Britain
by Amazon